This notebook belongs to

Printed in Great Britain
by Amazon

34532043R00068